Presented to

_____

On the occasion of

_____

From

_____

Date

_____

ISBN 1-57748-905-5

Published by Barbour Publishing, Inc., P. O. Box 719, Uhrichsville, Ohio 44683
http://www.barbourbooks.com

 Member of the
Evangelical Christian
Publishers Association

Printed in China.

MANY THANKS

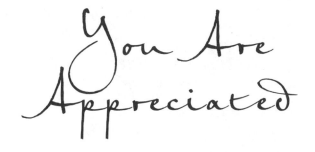

You Are Appreciated

Written and Compiled by
Ellyn Sanna

BARBOUR
PUBLISHING, INC.

*This is just to say,
"Thank you!"*

4–*Many Thanks*

1

The Priceless Gift
of Thanks

I urge you, first of all, to pray for all people. . . .
and give thanks.

1 TIMOTHY 2:1 NLT

$\mathcal{H}$ow can I ever say thank you for all that you have given me? What can a person do to repay someone for hours of understanding? You not only listened all those times when I was hurt or desperate, excited or glad, but you cried with me, you soothed my frustration, and you were more proud of me than I was of myself. Can I put a price on what that meant to me?

Of course I can't. What you have given me is not in the realm of finance and economy; instead, it belongs to the kingdom of God, to eternity. You gave yourself, with no thought of reward. What can I do but give myself in return? You have taught me just what being a friend is all about—and I can only pass that gift along, both to you and to the others in my life.

$\mathcal{G}$ratitude is one of those things
that cannot be bought.

LORD HALIFAX

$\mathcal{O}$ne can never pay in gratitude;
one can only pay "in kind"
somewhere else in life.

ANNE MORROW LINDBERGH

Thank You to Life's Quiet Teachers

As I greeted the guests at my wedding reception, a woman reached out and held my hands. She smiled at me, and I waited to hear her, "Congratulations." Instead, she quietly taught me a life-changing lesson.

"I remember when you were a young teenager," she said. "During those years I felt an urgency to pray for you, so I did."

She was one of my quiet teachers. Her words taught me that God cares enough about me to ask people outside my own family to pray for me.

The summer I was seven years old, a man from my church taught me another life-changing lesson. My family lived ten miles from our church, and we owned only one car, which my father used for work. This man lived only a couple of blocks from the church, and yet each day he drove the twenty-mile round-trip to take me to Vacation Bible School. He showed me that even as a child, my spiritual life was important to others in Christ's Body.

For the past thirty years a married couple I know has taught me another quiet lesson. Their spare bedroom is stacked high with boxes of gifts. These gifts aren't intended for their children or grandchildren; instead, this couple gives them to complete strangers. They hand them out at hospitals, prisons, universities, doctor's offices, and motels. They keep a gift tucked in her purse and another in the car, so that they are always prepared for a spontaneous chance to give. When anyone expresses an interest, the couple quietly offers one of these gifts—a New Testament. They have taught me to always be ready to give an answer for the hope within me.

All these quiet teachers have changed my life. They are common people who have taught me by their actions. Their lives demonstrate the importance of praying, serving, and sharing Scripture.

Each time I practice what they've taught me, my life is saying "thank you."

DONNA I. LANGE

$\mathcal{S}$weet is
the breath of vernal shower. . .
sweet music's melting fall, but sweeter yet
the still small voice of gratitude.

THOMAS GRAY

The poem speaks of "the still small voice of gratitude."
And, yes, I think it's true that the thankfulness I feel is
a little like God's own quiet voice. You've done so much
for me. Your acts have demonstrated God's love in con-
crete human form. And now I feel His Spirit breathe
softly through me as I say, "Thank you."

*A*nd though I ebb in worth,
I'll flow in thanks.

JOHN TAYLOR

I owe thee much:
Thou hast deserv'd from me
far, far beyond what I can ever pay.

ROBERT BLAIR

*T*here is no quality I would rather have,
and be thought to have,
than gratitude.

CICERO

The Reflection of Grace

The word gratitude comes from the same root word as grace. The root is a Latin word that means "free gift," "unearned pleasure or favor." We are not filled with gratitude when we are paid for a job well done or when we are recompensed for services rendered—or at least we do not feel the same sort of gratitude. No, our hearts are most grateful (another word that comes from the same Latin root) when someone does us a favor or bestows on us a gift for no other reason except love. Unmerited, undeserved, these gifts come into our life—just as God's grace does.

Gratitude is the human response to grace. It is the reflection that grace casts into our hearts.

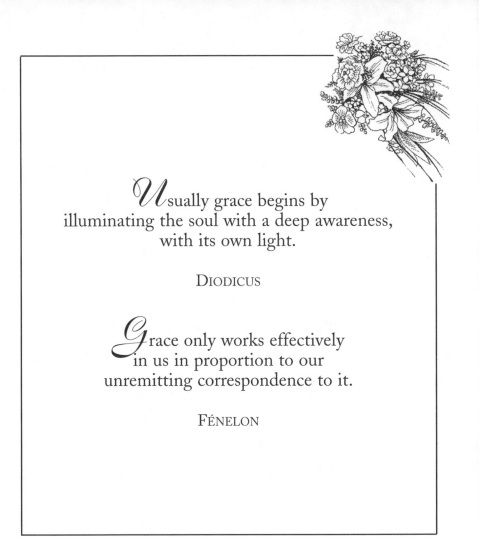

*U*sually grace begins by
illuminating the soul with a deep awareness,
with its own light.

DIODICUS

*G*race only works effectively
in us in proportion to our
unremitting correspondence to it.

FÉNELON

I'm so grateful for what you've done—
and so glad that you are you!
You've made a difference in my life.

A joyful and pleasant thing it is
to be thankful.

BOOK OF COMMON PRAYER

2

Too Great for Words

Many words are meaningless.

ECCLESIASTES 5:7 NIV

$\mathcal{I}$'d like to put into words just what I feel. I want to tell you how much you've helped me. Because of you, the world's a better place.

I really mean that. But my words seem so inadequate to express my gratitude. Even if I wrote a book about my feelings, in the end it would be little better than a signpost that points toward something else, something too big and wonderful to ever confine to words.

So in the end, what can I say except—thank you. You mean so much to me.

$\mathcal{W}$ords are but empty thanks.

COLLY CIBBER

*A*ccept my thought for thanks;
I have no words.

HANNAH MORE

*T*hough my mouth be dumb,
my heart shall thank you.

NICHOLAS ROWE

*O*ur words have wings,
but fly not where we would.

GEORGE ELIOT

The Mirror Inside Our Heads

The word thank comes from the same Old English root word that means "to think" and the Latin word for "thought." Perhaps those long-ago people who shaped our language understood that the external acts of others shape our thoughts even more than they do our outer lives. Acts of kindness may make our exterior lives easier and brighter—but the truly important and truly wonderful thing about kindness is how it changes our interior thoughts. When others express their love for us in action, our thoughts dwell on those actions. Our thinking becomes gentler, more vulnerable, more open to love from God and others.

Our mind is like an internal mirror, reflecting the outside world. And when others shape our world with kindness, the reflection in that mirror is changed as well.

The only words we have to express these thoughts are thank you.

3

Friendship's Foundation

*We give thanks to God always for you all,
making mention of you in our prayers.*

1 THESSALONIANS 1:2

What was it about you that drew me to you? I think it was simply that when I spoke about my feelings, you understood what I meant. We spoke the same language. I was so grateful to learn that I was not alone; someone else felt and thought as I did.

That understanding was the gift you gave before all others. Gratitude leapt up in my heart—and turned to friendship, a friendship that has endured ever since.

Friendships begin with. . .gratitude.

DANIEL DERONDA

The Beginning
of Friendship

It suddenly seemed to me that we had always been near each other, and that we would always be so. . . . It was one of those tender and peaceful feelings which are like a gift flowing from a region higher than ourselves, illuminating the future and deepening the present. From that moment our understanding was perfect. . . .

RAISSA MARITAIN,
We Have Been Friends Together

Thank you for your understanding!

awoke this morning with devout thanksgiving for my friends, the old and the new. Shall I not call God, the Beautiful, who daily showeth himself so to me in his gifts.

RALPH WALDO EMERSON

 f it were not for other people, we would be unable to grasp God's love for us. God comes to us in others, in those who reach out to us with the hands of friendship. Because human hands show us tenderness and care, we can comprehend a tender, caring Creator. He gives Himself to us through these ordinary people who are our friends.

And in return our hearts say, "Thank you."

*F*or this relief much thanks.

SHAKESPEARE,
Hamlet

*T*o give thanks is good, and to forgive.

ALGERNON CHARLES SWINBURNE

My gratitude does not mean I am in bondage to you now, weighed down with the sense of all I owe you. If that were so, then it would not be gratitude I felt, but an ordinary debt of money or service. No, what you have given to me came freely, as free as God's grace—and the gratitude that springs up in my heart does not tie me down but gives me wings.

Gratitude is lighter than a feather.

PLAUTUS

*N*o matter how shy you feel, I tell my kids, you can always say thank you. But sometimes it's hard to speak our thanks. "You shouldn't have," we say instead. "You did too much." Or, "Please. I don't deserve something so extravagant." Or we nod our heads brusquely and turn away, embarrassed to acknowledge what we've received.

What is it that gets in our way of accepting a gift? Is it our sense of unworthiness? Or at the opposite end of the spectrum, is it our pride? Either way, we're looking not at the gift, nor at the giver; instead, when we turn away from some gift, we're usually looking only at ourselves. Pride and embarrassment aren't so very different from each other; they're both self-conscious.

Thankfulness turns us outward, however. It takes the focus off ourselves. It allows us to reach out and accept what is given to us, simply, honestly, humbly.

And in the end the truest friendships are built on that simple, honest humility.

*T*o receive honestly is
the best thanks for a good thing.

GEORGE MACDONALD

*O*h, be my friend and teach me to be thine!

RALPH WALDO EMERSON

*G*ratitude is the most exquisite form
of courtesy.

JACQUES MARITAIN

Because of all the long talks we've had, because of all the ways you've supported me so many times, because of how you've taken time to be with me, I know that I have changed. All those little things you've done for me—and all the not so little, too—have helped me grow. You've helped me become a person I like being, the person God wants me to be. Thanks so much for everything!

Hand grasps hand,
    eye lights eye in good friendship,
And great hearts expand,
And grow. . . .

ROBERT BROWNING

I'm sorry for the times when I have been ashamed or embarrassed to express my gratitude. I am so very glad for all the gifts your friendship has given me.

Nothing is more honorable than
a grateful heart.

Seneca

4

The Joy of Memories

I thank my God upon every remembrance of you.

PHILIPPIANS 1:3

Looking back on my life, I find that you are woven into all my best memories. You were there on the days when I was so happy I felt as though I could fly. And you were also there when I felt as though my world was falling into pieces. Somehow your presence made the happy days even brighter and brought a sweetness even to the saddest moments of my life. When I remember those difficult times, I find that the memory of your support and understanding is stronger than the memory of my pain. Thank you for always being there for me.

Gratitude is the memory of the heart.

JEAN BAPTISTE MASSIEU

*O*ne day held
the memory of you. . .
and sowed the sky with
tiny clouds of love.

RUPERT BROOKE

*N*ever shall I forget the days
which I spent with you.

LUDWIG VAN BEETHOVEN

I cannot but remember such things were,
that were most precious to me.

SHAKESPEARE

I have a room whereinto
no one enters
Save I myself alone:
There sits a blessed memory on a throne.

CHRISTINA ROSSETTI

Memories are very private things, a personal storehouse of treasures and sorrows. What a gift God gave us when He created our brains with the ability to remember!

At night sometimes when I can't sleep, or on a long trip when my mind wanders over the past as I gaze out at the road, I think back on my favorite memories, the ones that make me smile or even laugh out loud. And my heart is full of gratitude. "Thank you," I whisper. "Thank you."

The river of time sweeps on, but there, like a tree planted by the water, is our Lord Jesus Christ. He became man, willing to plant himself by the river of time.

AUGUSTINE

When I reflect on my past, I'm surprised to see the ways God worked out the details of my life. At the time, events seemed chaotic and out of control; and yet looking back, I see now the pattern being woven. At the center of my memories, again and again I find Christ, "planted like a tree" by time's swirling river.

And many times He used you to help me find direction in my life. I am so thankful for all my memories of you.

$\mathcal{T}$hanks for the memory. . . .

LEO ROBIN

$\mathcal{T}$hank you so much for all the memories you have given me. I will never forget what you have meant to me. You're so easy to remember!

5

The Language of Heaven

In every thing give thanks:
for this is the will of God in Christ Jesus
concerning you.

1 THESSALONIANS 5:18

*S*aying thank you is not some debt we pay to God and others, an obligation, a cultural courtesy. No, expressing our gratitude is much more important than that. In fact, the Bible indicates that it is essential to our spiritual well-being.

The thankful heart accepts that it is not the center of the world. It acknowledges its dependency on others. Humility and thankfulness walk hand in hand, and love springs from their union.

Thanksgiving is
the language of heaven, and we had
better start to learn it if we are not to be mere
dumb aliens there.

J. GOSSIP

For the invasion of my soul
  by Thy Holy Spirit:
For all human love and goodness
  that speak to me of Thee:
For the fullness of Thy glory outpoured
  in Jesus Christ
I give Thee thanks, O God.

JOHN BAILLIE

$\mathcal{N}$ow thank we all our God,
With heart and hands and voices
Who wondrous things has done,
In whom this world rejoices,
Who, from our mothers' arms,
Hath blessed us on our way
With countless gifts of love,
And still is ours today.

MARTIN RINKART
(trans. Catherine Winkworth)

$\mathcal{L}$et me praise you for these things, my God who made them all, but do not let the love of them be like glue to fix them to my soul.

AUGUSTINE

$\mathcal{A}$s we say thank you to those who have done so much for us, we must never forget to look beyond them to the Giver of all gifts, our Creator God. He is the Source of all good, and His love speaks through human kindness. Our every breath should be filled with gratitude, for He has given us everything.

$\mathcal{I}$f the things of this world delight you, turn your love to their Creator.

AUGUSTINE

*T*hanks be to you, Jesus Christ,
For the many gifts Thou hast
bestowed on me. . . .
I am giving Thee worship with
my whole life,
I am giving Thee assent with my whole power,
I am giving Thee praise with my whole tongue,
I am giving Thee honour with my whole utterance.

CARMINA GADELICA

I pray that God will help me to live my life in constant gratitude, my whole being offered up in thankful humility.

And I thank God every day for making you!